THE DARK SAFEKEEPING

THE DARK SAFEKEEPING

GLORIA NIXON-JOHN

MAYAPPLE PRESS 2022

Published by   Mayapple Press
                    362 Chestnut Hill Road
                    Woodstock, NY 12498
                    mayapplepress.com

ISBN 978-1-952781-11-7
Library of Congress Control Number 2022932259

ACKNOWLEDGEMENTS

Some of these poems have appeared in: *A3 Review and Press of London; Bangalore Review; BeyondWords; Clover a Literary Rag; Free Spirit Anthology; Green Prints; Local Honey, Midwest; Moonstone Arts Center; Ogham Stone of Ireland; Poets Choice Anthology; River Teeth; Temenos Literary Journal of Central Michigan University; Tiny Seed; Wanderlust; Wayne State University Review; Wingless Dreamer, Iron City.*

Dedicated to my students then and now
and life's unlikely teachers.

To the lost, imprisoned, suffering, and forgotten
of my species and all other species.

Cover design by Judith Kerman based on photo of Moonflower by Bob Peterson (*plants.ces.ncsu.edu*), used under Creative Commons. Photo of author by Renee. Book designed and typeset by Judith Kerman with text and titles in Perpetua.

CONTENTS

The Cats of Castle Yard   5
Excitement on Death Row   6
In Our Sights   8
Prison Bullfrog   10
Mouse Soup   11
A Winter Morning   12
Far Enough   13
Rat   14
Library Fish   15

Document Enough   19
For Reggie 1971-2009   20
For All Who Think I Am Sleeping   21
Show Horses   22
The Rhetoric of Skunk   24
Lost White Cat   25
On the 401   26
Last Night   27
I Promised to Send You a Poem in March   28
In the Shadow of Medusa   29
In the Hollows   30
Refusal   31
It Is Raining in Venice   32
Practicing Verbs at the Tomb of Michelangelo   33
Into the silent water she went   *34*
A Thin Poem   35
For My Friend Behind the Drawn Curtain   38
There is a place   39
Memories of Love Lost   40
Last Call   41
Only May   43
Before the Rain   44
After an October Rain   45
Champagne Campaign   46
Convenience Store 2020   47
The Mighty Allegheny 1601*   48
The Vultures of Gettysburg   50
Gettysburg Gift Shop Painting   51

Onions   55
Red Peppers   57
Oakland County   58
One Last Time   59
Fore   60
In 8th Grade   62
When I Stand Watching   63
Until They Fall   64

In June   69
At the Tire Repair Shop   71
Pedicure Time   73
The young barista   74
I Join Them   76
Hugs   77
Come Child, I Am Waiting   79
Grandma   81
If I Am Ever in a Coma   82
It's All Too Much   84

About the Author   86
Acknowledgments: 87

"You can cage the singer but not the song."
Harry Belafonte

"Putting a man's life to waste is not justice."
Kenneth Eade

THE CATS OF CASTLE YARD

For the inmates of the Kentucky State Penitentiary

A visitor to the prison,
I am surprised to see
dozens of them muster
into the prison yard,
some from drainpipes,
others up and over the outside wall,
their soft agility defying
the rolling maze of barbed wire.

Most are striped, the guard says.
A mold cast centuries before,
a speck of gold in their eyes
from Blue Ridge foxes.

The odd one out, mostly white
with just a blaze of black
above bottle-green eyes, paces
like an expectant father
near the riveted door until
a bell rings and the iron rolls   and
the men stream out, neat in khaki shirts
and trousers, a spool of pale ribbon
unwinding—they might be monks
or factory men holding to routine.

The piebald cat stretches his neck,
discriminates, not that one, not this,
the small head a metronome
until his awaited steps out
of the dark passage, drops to one knee,
touches the singular acceptance,
the arching, breaking grace.

Excitement on Death Row

When Jessie saw two
chrysalises of jade and gold
hanging from a ledge in his cell,
he became a sentry, a spy
to the coming out—could not
sleep or read—would not
leave his cell, so compelled
to witness the wonder.

Exhausted, days later
he fell asleep, and missed
the last chance metamorphoses.
(The shame and loss he felt
was hard to reckon, became
just one more possibility
stolen from him.)

The monarchs soared and lighted,
anointed common things.
Wings opened and closed
in a syncopation that reminded
him of grandpa's squeeze box.

More monarchs emerged,
joined in.
Soon the guards came
with nets on long poles
to capture the stealthier
monarchs that swarmed, lifted,
then dispersed like confetti.

Day after day the men took bets
that the monarchs would escape
the guards, who were unaccustomed
to capturing anything without
guns, clubs, Tasers and trickery.

It was particularly satisfying
to see the flying kaleidoscope
weave in and out of the locked
cells in a Kabuki dance of sorts
before they gathered in a flutter,
lifting up and out through a small breach
in an untended gate, out
into the yard, then up and up
toward the necessary
unction of sun and sky.

In Our Sights

For Leif

Prisoner 836-770 writes,
The prison was on lockdown
all weekend because of a fight
in the yard. I had to take a
bird bath in my sink,
had to jog in my cell, finally
read the book of poetry you sent.

He said he liked a poem
by Stephen Dunn, about the time
Dunn asked his students to write
about their sacred place
and many of them wrote
about being in a moving car,
music playing, a companion along.

Prisoner 836-770 said the poem
reminded him of days long ago
when he would drive into the country
around Lexington, past farms,
where horses ran along the fence
as he passed, the feeling that he
was running with them
up and over the pasture gate.

Further along, he tells of a story
he heard on NPR, a story about
a spacecraft designed to collide
with a comet, to send pictures
in real-time, back down to earth
the purpose of this unclear.

The thought of distant objects
colliding offers me relief
from his walled-in sorrow,
relief from barbed assurances,

away from the key-keeper's clanging
sanctimony, the obtuse injustice
of the unseen starlit sky.

But sorrow is a useless act.
Better to hop into my car, imagine
Prisoner 836-770 along,
take to the open highway
radio blasting, Bowie singing
Ground Control to Major Tom—

                                    a comet just barely in our sights.

Prison Bullfrog

He usually writes about his routine,
rises before 5 a.m. to weak coffee,
scrubs floors, paints walls,
one hour in the exercise yard,
or a dream from the night before:
a fishing trip with his father long dead.

Today he writes about the bullfrog
in the alley behind his cell.
It has survived winter,
has emerged from a weep hole
in a retaining wall, so large now
it may not fit into the hole for long.

He reports that management
cut down a rose bush
that has graced the yard for years.
Take heart, he writes, *they cut
only the stems, didn't know enough
to dig out the roots.*

It is usually his regret that stays
with me long after the letter,
but today it is the frog embodied
in the small round rock that I excise
from my garden, a damp bulk
that I lift toward the sun.

I give the rock legs, long and lithe
ready to leap out and over—over,
up toward the warm light,
but his heaviness resists,
draws inward, hardens
into the dark safekeeping.

MOUSE SOUP

Prisoner #45978 writes,
I touched it with my spork
and it was cooked.
One of the guards took
a picture of it to share
with others for a good laugh.
The prison report
of the incident did not include
a photograph of the mouse
in a bowl of soup;
the newspaper report
spared the shock as
Administrator Jones
chortled and explained,
"If not for the distress
it caused those to whom
it was served up,
it might have been
a work of art at MOMA—
call it 'Mouse in Soup circa 2020.'"
All in all, he concluded
that there was no need
for further inspection.

A Winter Morning

For Angelina

I fill the winter feeder
with sunflower seeds,
corn, orange rind—then
watch from the window.
A cardinal is the first to come;

I see his masked face
in the bare lilac bush.
His wind-swept pompadour
makes me laugh.

This is his cameo appearance.
He peck-pecks, then lifts his head,
as intense as a sommelier
until he notices me, levitates,
aims for the thicket—is gone.

I take up my field glasses,
point and focus into the tree line,
look for his feet of pink twine,
listen for his minor key—
whoit-whoit-whoit.

Instead, I hear sweeter songs,
a warble, *trill-tweet*.
I spy brown wings, the soft blue
underbelly of a thrasher,
the dusty near hue of him—
the red of twigs and winterberries.
But all else that comes in red
is never so red as he.

Far Enough

My bluetick brought it home,
dropped it on the front step,
then slinked away
as if to say *this is what I do;*
take it or leave it.

Its breathing labored,
spine an unnatural arc,
small black claws scraping
to get to anywhere else.

Young woodchuck
or possum? Too young
for distinction and I
couldn't look closely,
would see all of life there.

Instead I placed him in a soft
shady spot with a breeze,
couldn't do anything else.
It was all too late,
tableau in a crystal ball.

The next morning, he was still
as I knew he would be.
My pallbearer husband
went with gloves and spade,
an undertaker's deliberate stride

       to dig a small hole—far enough
       from our mutable fortune
       where the groundswell
       will first flatten then
       welcome the dark roots.

Rat

Besides love and sympathy, animals exhibit
other qualities connected with the social instincts
which in us would be called moral.

Charles Darwin

I am in the barn tossing hay
when he paints a quick gray line across my path,
then bottom up and down
                    into the throat of a hole.

I should have been repulsed, you say?
Disease after all, and the tiny shining eyes,
hairless trailing whip of tail too much the texture of tongue.
Most find him repugnant, yet he stirs a strange wonder in me
and so I do not back away—stay quietly waiting,
long enough to see him lift first the tiny thimbled nose,
then the carefully chiseled head
                    up into the vigilant light.

Tomorrow someone else will come with shovel,
poison, a bucket of water to drown him,
a rock to block his escape.
And so, I tell him—go with god,
god of nimble feet, of whiskered sniffing snout,
god with the smallest all-seeing eye that
                    looks down into holes.

LIBRARY FISH

For the Black Pacu

Whose idea was it to put him
in an aquarium just three times his length?
I wonder if he remembers diving and surfacing,
                    pushing forward and forward against white water

toward a cerulean sea. Instead of this staccato jetting
around green plastic plants,
the glass abatement like hexed water
where he must twist
like a turnstile just to reverse.

Children look in, poke the glass,
laugh at his underbite,
his pin-sharp teeth
that he would use in the wild
only if there was blood.
He is an amusement—all but the carnival music.
The librarian sees my concern,
tells me the Pacu is content;
this is all he has known for fifteen years.
I don't believe it
any more than I believe in internment camps.

I want to ask, what is his crime?
But if I stand at a certain distance,
look long enough, I will see the soft flutter
of his smoky gray scales,
a glint of gold filigree close to bone,
and I can imagine him far
                    and deep and free
                              well beyond this stagnant light.

"The wind of Heaven is that which blows
between a horse's ears."
Bedouin Proverb

Document Enough

For Blacker and Eli

There are no words
to use to bury a horse
no airs above ground
no hoof beat

      full stop.

These are the tinny vowels
(I have no need for them)
throw them down the dark well

useless coins.

These are the consonants
blue-winged flies buzzing

      dull twigs breaking underfoot.

No words, just the once lofty
once muscled phrases lying flat
against the impervious earth
where his last long longest breath

      is document enough.

FOR REGGIE 1971–2009

I walk down to the barn
just before the sky opens,
before the human noises say
Be sad   Be joyful
want everything
want nothing at all.

This one horse comes forward,
an unexpected grace,
his greeting soft castanets
before he lowers his head, asks
for a soft stroke against
the deepening curve,
asks for a scratch
under his flaxen mane.

All purpose measured
by the fading stars,
the rising sun,
a handful of sweet feed
that opens the sky.

FOR ALL WHO THINK I AM SLEEPING

For Jessica, majestic Arabian

Well before dawn I walk
the dark path to the barn.
I have left the tucked surfaces,
the rumble of sleeping cats,
to find myself beside you
under the marbled moon.

Years ago we rode as one,
muscle and mayhem
over the teeming fields,
clucking, nickering,
pulse on pulse,
shadow over water
                reflecting sky.

In this light we might both be young again,
the end so much like the beginning,
all bone and wisp unsteady bending,
nibble-nibbling the sweet grasses
as daintily now as sipping tea.

Back there in the dark house
I was thinking of time, of things brand new—
of then, of would have been. But here
there is only the space we fill,
one source of light compared to another,
a surface to walk on, plentiful or barren.

Back there in the dark house
they believe I am sleeping,
that you are taking leave. Yet
they cannot know how the moment
comes tottering forward holding
something bitter enough to give,
sweet enough to take away.

Show Horses

They once stormed the Great Plains,
all hoof-beat dusty-thunder,
reared and reveled untethered,
snorts and whinnies thrown
into the ungirded wind.

And now to see this one
so silent, so contained,
curried then buffed,
his mane a dull linear cut.

He is boxed in, his legs pretend
at a trot before he kicks,
splits a board in his stall,
all this for Jody who has
the perfect boots and breeches,
her hair collected into a snood,
her perky ass tucked up
into a perfect seat.

      Go introduce yourself
      before the main event,
      scratch under his mane,
      exhale into his nostrils,
      let him take in your scent
      and he will never forget you.

      Before you walk away,
      look again, look into his eyes,
      eyes capable of a 350-degree view
      and the ability to take a telescopic
      measure of any distant menace.

      Tell me what you see
      reflected in his eyes.
      The rolling field beyond

the well-tended fences?
The never ending mercurial
 sky? No. Instead you see
a blunted view—just you
standing there with all
of your good intentions.

THE RHETORIC OF SKUNK

It is March when
the black and white unsteadiness
(like a child writing cursive
for the first time)
      crosses my path
      on the parchment
      of melting snow.

          Frozen vowels simmer
          up from the bottom of the pond,
          fricatives slide across
                    branch and bud.

Yet who of us knows spring
as you do, can die
yet send the message
that you have died?
No other.

Not King, not Emissary,
screen star, not hero
or villain will imbue
as you do—Skunk.

Lost White Cat

It is hard to find you
in February
when the snow
is melting

into promises of   flank   or   ear,

                            there

      or here.

We were a pair, you and me,
the warmth and whirr of you
against my anchored aching bones.

       Come home!

              Come home!

Then March begins brazen,
swirling, licking at the rusting gate,
the ancient tree limbs' shadows fall

as I call

      youeee

         Kitty!

           Kit-tee!

And nearly to the instant of that first mild wind
I will notice stars now closer here than you,
a sentient spring will surface,
the crocus will grow you a paw.

ON THE 401

For Bronwen

On the 401 near Coulborne
I pass a semi carrying hogs.
Their noses scope the portholes,
large pink buttons sewn on steel.

I expected to see cows
in a Playschool puzzle pose,
the calm sadness
that is always in their eyes,
to realize them whole
one last time.

I didn't expect the raw of pigs,
their plumped skins begging
a consummate forgiveness,
easily split wide open
like a woman's lip.

Last Night

I heard the proverbial bump,
scramble of predator and prey.
Rabbit fleeing a winged shadow,
coyote in the neighbor's coop?

In the morning I learned
it was an inside job—
a thimble-sized heart on
the pantry shelf,
silver viscous over
three crimson chambers.

I placed it in my palm—wondered
why the predator ate snout,
tail and gristle, not
this most tender part.

Perhaps it was a gift, a word
from the world that shares
my space, a reminder
from one animal to another
of sacrifice, of shared survival.

I Promised to Send You a Poem in March

For Holly

My apologies as I flip
the calendar to April, but
the red-winged blackbird
has distracted me.

The small red blaze
on his wing is the flame
of the Sacred Heart of Jesus
that the nuns proctored

in Catechism long ago
when all we wanted
was to jump
in the spring puddles. And

high above the cornfield
the red-tailed hawk has opened
his wings like a book, revealing
an underside of dark lines,
impossible to read from earth.

You must excuse my friends
who call to invite me to lunch.
I explain I have a poem to write.
"That can't be hard," one says.
"Call when you're free."

But it is not easy to be free
of poems even as my feet turn
toward spring puddles
and my eyes lift toward wings,

until a ridge of buds appears
on the branches of the forsythia,
an unrepentant ellipsis
that gives me pause for spring.

IN THE SHADOW OF MEDUSA

Because of the Biblical rains,
they move indoors early this year.
Flies and mosquitoes circle, annoy,
slugs traverse up walls and windows,
their cryptic messages in filmy cursive.

Mother, I remember how you
wrapped the broom in rags to pull
cobwebs down, how you burned
tomato bugs until they popped.

In the shadow of Medusa, you searched
for a new way to tie up your hair
like Lucille Ball or Gloria Swanson,
you searched for some way
to bury the warnings that came to us,
like the kitten born with only one large eye.

Mother, the cobwebs are finely spun
in my closet, the spider willy-nills
across the margins of this page
as I think about windows you
never opened, the space you
never cluttered with need.

In the Hollows

At the kitchen sink
her hands rise up
through soapy water,
a disjointed life form
extinct eons ago.

Her grandmother
stood there too,
praised Jesus, praised
a new deal coming—coming
up out of buried coal.

Her mama looked to
the mountain beyond, said
it touched heaven's door,
clear cut last week, sliced
down to a bald plateau.

She keeps a stone in
her pocket, worries it
round and smooth,
blind eye of the philosopher
in a foreign tableau.

Her skin is milky, thin,
no one writes of her
or fights her wars,
not here where the earth
dips down, hollows low

where history is nonplussed
and struggle is all she will know.

Refusal

Tonight, the waitress tells us it is tradition
to kiss the moose head anchored to the wall
at Sledder's Bar and Grill—antlers, face and neck
caught while turning back toward
the sun-drenched forest of his legs.

Just last week while walking the long finger
of land that divides the Bay, I met a nurse
who spoke about a patient, *just a kid*, she said,
who asked her time and time again to scratch
his missing foot, pointed down as if it
was a fish thrashing in a bucket.

But this is not a poem about war or missing limbs;
it is about the child who, when asked to kiss
the moose head, refused to consider the part
as the whole, who tore away—running, running,
caught at the door in a snare of arms.

And this is about what we wish to offer
this child, that she might accept
the disjointed decorum, ignore
the horror we see as sanctuary,
celebrate the histrionics
of what we make grave.

IT IS RAINING IN VENICE

For Carmine

It is raining in Venice
and I am alone.
The empty gondolas bob
their lacquered bodies,
collide and groan.

Yesterday in a café near San Marco,
when Carmine saw the bill for our drinks,
he taught me the word for "thief."
Ladro, ladra, he said,
his tongue rolling the r,
bubbles breaking the surface.
I tried and my tongue made the sound
of a poorly shuffled deck of cards.

Thief, I told him, *the-ee-ff*
close the word at the end.
First there is a breeze,
then a ride of vowel.
Think of the final sound
as a soft protest, a tickle
of air over your bottom lip,
gentle but final.
He tried the word:
theefha, allora, I can no stopah
with effah.

We laughed until there were tears,
a laugh that came from a holding,
lifting, opening place.

It is raining in Venice
and I am now alone,
where words move up and on like vapor,
where the moon has been sinking
for two thousand years.

Practicing Verbs at the Tomb of Michelangelo

I consider the conjugation
of "to be": *to have, essere, avere.*
Someday I will be dead
but Michelangelo has death.
Death lives with him
just as marble weeps
and the ages gnash their teeth.

My Florentine cousin asks,
"Do you know Michelangelo?"
He thinks of my spinning
in the Sears Tower, shopping
at The Mall of America,
driving a big machine.

When he notices my tears,
afraid he has insulted me,
he gasps, as if to remove
his words from the air,
his face the Centaur
in *Pallade e il Centauro*.

For a moment, I want out
of my flesh—this life—
want to be a cool shapeless
substance in the hands
of Michelangelo.

Instead, I say, *essere, avere*
at the tomb of Michelangelo.

Into the silent water she went

with no shoes, no earrings, no scarf;
someone urged me to look away, but
I needed to see her one more time,
to notice how the sea encircled her
then became still once again.

       And nothing was sent in her place
       —now there is only quiet
       and more of the same.

As we mourned, one empty conch
scrolled like an ear,
gave a hollow respite
for this life above.

       The eulogy handed round—
       waves when they came
       brought relief. Yet

the surface of all things dry
wanted what she had.
O sea and land and sea again,
send something up to the surface—
bubbles that live on the instant,

a periwinkle or blue Iris,
to breathe her a sky.

A THIN POEM

For Marilyn

I

At the memorial
your remains
rendered
in ash
in a brass box
small enough
for recipe cards
the irony
not lost
on any of us
your fleshiness
reduced to
this   and
wouldn't
you have
been
the first
to laugh
to celebrate
the rate
at which
the cursed
excessiveness
fell finally   and
so easily
from bone
to marvel at
the graceful
sizzle the
dribble drizzle pop
a light tune against
the heavy dirge
a nimble dance
smoke rising

before the finite
the effortless
settling in
easy as pie
piece of cake
crumbs of
the new
un-girded
you.

II

I try to
reconfigure you
in Louie's Café
on payday
ordering
au jus,
crepe suzette,
a *rissole.*
Your birthday
in Greek Town,
your excessive
floppy brimmed hat,
shouting *Opa!*
too close to the flames,
shouting *more wine!*
I try to reconfigure you
from my own
fleshy hands
fastening this
to that
around your
new
configuration,
toiling
as the living do,
adding this
futility

on top of that,
trying
for blood
and bone,
flesh and flesh
unable to reckon
the new
small-time
you
in the eternity
of a box.

For My Friend Behind
the Drawn Curtain

I place the vase of flowers
on the table nearest her bed,
then offer her the wildflower
that a child has sent,
the wildflower still clutching
crumbs of soil and wilted so
it makes us laugh.

They will take my hand tomorrow, she says
as she lifts the doomed hand
up into the sterile hospital light,
the loose skin over bone,
raised veins suddenly beautiful.
Or should I let the poison spread?
she says, opening and closing
the hand like a warning light.

Then, *please*, she says, *oh please*
(the rabbit's foot already caught in the trap).

I can see that she wants to burrow
under the blankets as she
might burrow deep into the rooted dark,
wants to dream this all away, but
the indelible visions behind her eyes
make dreaming impossible.

Forced as a friend to bear witness,
I confess to a private longing
for an early spring, for the promise
of the regenerative stem,
for the miracle of bud and bloom.

THERE IS A PLACE

just before the alfalfa field dips
toward a stand of locust
where Potawatomi once walked
toward the sound of water
as it yodeled over rock.

I have walked there too
looking for wildflowers,
for berries, for answers
I didn't expect to find.

Once into the tangle
of old growth limbs,
some thriving some fallen,
I hear the truth
that leaf offers sky

about who once was,
who will come next,
about how the buried
will be unearthed.
I tell you this because you

are here—now, between
memory and longing.

MEMORIES OF LOVE LOST

Forgetting is silk—
still I choose the chafe
of memory. Today I am
raw with it.

Sometimes I can keep memory
in its place—an unopened shoebox.
Celluloid faces and fingers
push up against the dusty lid.

One memory grows arms, legs,
lifts itself up and into
an empty freight car—
the rhythm on the tracks
a heartbeat taking leave.

Another memory boils
white hot, fuming, flows
unencumbered, covers
everything despite all
futile attempts to escape.

And even as he stands
in the distance, his hands
like two starfish reaching,
telling me to remember
this, remember that,
asking for an element
heavier than air—still

I can only offer smoke
and ash.

Last Call

For Jim

The afternoon you called—
water boiling on the stove,
towels in the dryer—
I said I had to keep it short.

You asked how I was doing,
the acquiescence in your voice
an old familiar warning.
I pictured you poking
around in volcanic ash
as if doing so would get us
back to fire somehow.

What do you want?
was all I could say. After all,
it had taken me a decade to learn
how to refuse the stones
you handed me for jewels.

More small talk—too much,
until the conversation
tasted of burnt toast.
Jim, don't, I said.
*The dryer has stopped, and
the pot is boiling over.*

Still you reminded me
of three good years,
parties in the San Fernando Valley,
how a pleading Janis Joplin
called, *come on, come on, take it!*
How she made dervishes of us all.

Remember, you said,
your voice going fuzzy
like a radio station too far away,

the day you got lost in Tuna Canyon?
Remember you walked off after
a butterfly you said was the color
of saffron and sky?

I had trouble finding you. Remember?
The echo off the mountains
made it seem like you were close
but you had walked miles—
lost and limping, cursing me
by the time I found you.

I don't tell him that I
remember being surprised
as the butterfly disappeared,
first into the open limbs
of blue elderberry,
then out of reach—gone,
saffron and blue burned
into the setting sun.

That was your last call;
you were dead a week later,
dead before I had the chance
to call you back, to tell you
what I remember most
about the day in Tuna Canyon
is the easy way you let go
of my hand as I took chase.

Only May

It is only May and already we
complain about the heat. The lilac
and the big leaf maple make us
      zig
              zag
                          toward obligation.

Last night a moth got in
through that one open window,
thumped inside an abandoned shoe,
forced me to move the corners round,
to think about meadows heavy with light.

But today out on the open highway
a duck and ducklings scatter
like bowling pins, warn
of some measure of deception,
some existential need that tells
the mulberry to grow
first this way, then that.

BEFORE THE RAIN

He died before the rain
water filled his fishing boat,
water that reflected
a flawless sky
when there should
have been clouds.

His wife called the items
left in the boathouse junk—she
wanted all of it, including
the boat, hauled away.

But his old coonhound
sat near the boat for days,
staring out at the lake
as if he was expecting
Jesus or at least a blue trout
to come sliding ashore.

AFTER AN OCTOBER RAIN

Can you hear the geese
tell us all to gather,
sonics slightly ahead of wind?

Below, the swan asks a question
with her satin neck
and white on white;
the lily pad is happy
to die for change,
to sink politely
under the season.

We are the swirl-between
as the geese fly over,
their imperfect arrowhead
sharper than our sharpest part.

And even if you were to
blindfold me I would go too,
would not ask why.

Think of it—we could be envoy
instead of saber or cave, a movement
free to make the tiniest circumscribed part
as important as the whole.

CHAMPAGNE CAMPAIGN

First the pop and pour,
CO_2 rushing to the surface,
then *scoreggia* a sound
that makes Italian schoolboys laugh.

Some plosives streak upward
disguised as vowels, some
stop on the surface,
consonants falling flat.

The VIPs gather. One suggests
bigger flutes, another remarks
how each bubble contains
a rainbow even while clouds
threaten, a surrogate notes
how a good number cling,
shimmy, rise up, implode.

And really now, what choice
do we have but to lift
the tempest to our lips
and wait for polite acceptance
(with reciprocity, of course).

Finally, the empty chalice
is hurled in a measured arch
of celebration of discontent.

Convenience Store 2020

In the time of Covid

Nine months in I begin
to feel like prey—fear
leaping up dropping off
like a near miss on I-94.

Lonely, I venture out
to the convenience store,
a small store, little danger
save for Muzac, fluorescent
pestilence buzzing, tinting
exposed skin unearthly blue.

(Flat line blue—call it—)

I try to walk wide circles
around the others when
a child comes close, looks up,
smiles, and all I can think
is, *where is her mask?*

Suddenly everyone is too close,
their mouths are covered
but I see their breath
puff up their masks, see them
touch shelves, shopping basket,
money, hands everywhere
with air and spittle that can leap up,
latch on, burrow in—kill.

Then the horror of a face,
arms reaching just behind me
in the door of the dairy cooler,
fear a racing racket in my ears—
until I see—the face is me,

both predator and prey.

THE MIGHTY ALLEGHENY 1601*

See my iron stirrups that bid you
ride straddle into the hills of Ohio,
the mountains of Tennessee.
I see all with my Cyclops's eye
and my hoot is as true
as the iron toll of Katie Liberty

Listen to me

Pity the curious farm boy
who dared to jump a ride,
got too close to the tracks,
tumbled off like a pumpkin
where his most fertile seed
will sprout beside the tracks
of twenty-five tons of the 1601.

Listen to me

           Listen to me

When I tell you my sound
will make your granddaughter sad,
you need not stop a stranger
on the street to say
Listen to that lonely sound.
He carries the inheritance of lonely.

Listen to me

           Listen to me

                      Listen to me

Yes, there is something comical
about my last flash of red
as if to say: the joke's on you—
like a presidential hoot,
puff of promises against

the winding freedom that flattens
the Indian Head nickel
you place so carefully
on the tracks.

*There are only two Allegany Locomotives left. I was inspired by
the one at the Henry Ford Museum in Livonia, Michigan.*

THE VULTURES OF GETTYSBURG

On occasion visitors to Gettysburg
have witnessed a kettle of vultures
collect near the battleground.

Those early pundits,
inky hand historians,
hawkers, gawkers high
in the tower of the next day
proclaim the battle less
important than the speech.

And we believe them,
come to hear the words
scored and trimmed
to the beat of fife and drum
when a young boy high
on his father's shoulders
uses his whole arm to point up.

Their guide pauses from
the memorized telling,
notices the vultures.
Oh yes, they come every year
around the date—the time
of the major battle. Odd.

Her words lack surprise,
still all attention goes up
to the trees to see the oddity
she has dismissed,

the boy's arm now a muzzle,
eyes searching up to parapet
and tree toward the feathered vagrants
hunched with intent—vultures
brought by a recalcitrant DNA
for the blood of Plum Run,
to feast, feast on self-evident belief.

GETTYSBURG GIFT SHOP PAINTING

General Longstreet's
head turns away from Pickett.
Both accede to the impending
slaughter, while

a celestial light anoints
the horses, their ears pricked,
nostrils flared, haunches yielding,
ready to gallop forward
without prejudice.

"We are our stories. We tell them to stay alive or keep alive those who only live now in the telling."
Niall Williams, "History of Rain"

Onions

I see him from the dining room
where I sit with my laptop.
What a nice guy, I am thinking,
out there in this intolerable heat,
weeding my vegetable garden.
He is sweat-drenched, wearing
one of those Lawrence of Arabia hats.

But what is he throwing
into the wheelbarrow,
round with tails trailing behind
like tiny meteors?
I can't see the lifting up
but know the garden plat.
He is next to the rhubarb—onions!

He is pulling up onions,
his action so cavalier, like a young boy
learning to pitch underhand.
I know he is well intentioned;
still, I bolt out the door.
"What are you throwing away?
What? Are those my onions?"

"The tops are all dry," he says.
"Those are onions! They keep growing
underground. They get bigger!"
Later I take them from the wheelbarrow,
cradle them in the sling I have made
with the bottom of my blouse—
a wasteful garnish for tonight's salad.

Such an attachment to onions.
But the story is that my grandfather,
fearing there were no onions in America,
lined his steamer trunk with them

before he left the port of Naples.
He guarded that trunk on the long journey
in the dark hull of steerage.

He guarded the trunk
near spittoon and privy,
a lean-to for sitting,
a surface for playing cards,
the sweet stink of those onions
his only certainty,
talisman against change.

The trunk, now mine, still carries
the faint odor of onions,
and always, before I slice one open,
I think of each opalescent surface
growing layer after layer,
some finally as large
as Grandfather's determined fist.

RED PEPPERS

He is proud when he hands me
three red peppers for roasting.
They are a red alert
in my white kitchen—
his Cheshire grin tells me he knows
the gesture is a mix of gift and imposition.

This is an easy way to please him—
I slice the pepper in half lengthwise,
remove the pulp and seeds,
flatten them on the grill, turn the broiler to HI.
The scent is both bitter and sweet.

My mother, dead for twenty-nine years,
stands next to me at the stove,
apron around her shoulders like a harness.
Faded roses climb from a rickrack hem.

I want to tell her to take the apron off,
to throw it down, to run from the stove,
but the truth is I would give anything
to see her standing just as she did.

Once the peppers are cooled,
I remove the blackened skins.
The exposed flesh is slack,
moist, more pink than red,
like that most private flesh.

I soak them in olive oil and garlic
before I place them on the plate
that Mother bought
with S&H Green Stamps.

Later, I will hold them up,
an offering that he will put
into his mouth and tell me
how good they are.

OAKLAND COUNTY

Here in the richest of counties,
in the polish of a Sunday afternoon,
the sky swirls blue and blossoms
along the hedge's rust.

In the polish of a Sunday afternoon,
sculpted lawns and shammied sedans
along the hedges rust
as a sprinkler spurts a rainbow.

Sculpted lawns and shammied sedans
while expansive porches are empty.
A sprinkler spurts a rainbow
and each sky and mood grows grayer.

While expansive porches are empty
and windowless faces grow grayer
despite hedge or hybrid or hemp,
the golden riches soon tarnish

and windowless faces grow grayer
as they chant their beveled desires.
The gardener hides his leafy dreams
here in the richest of counties.

ONE LAST TIME

I am reading
in the room adjacent
to where he sits
watching TV,
the sportscaster
breaking his heart.
Damn, damn, damn! he says.
The big black dog
at his feet is content
even with his discontent.

I have shouted to him
to turn the volume down—
this is what we do,
shout about volume,
mumble our petty annoyances,
ignore the fleeting
tender looks.

High above in the darkening sky
one hopeful star offers
a tender light

one last time
a million years ago.

FORE

It was the good people of Meohmy, Michigan, who, upon realizing that they needed a golf course and further realizing that they had used up all of their land building fast-food chains and mini-malls, decided to build a golf course over the old cemetery. The city council was amused to think about introducing the concept of "fore" to the dead.

The dead were not amused.

The notion especially angered Mr. Webb, dead for a century, killed when a horse and buggy veered to avoid hitting a cow. And the forever young Miss Maloney, who choked at age twenty on a chicken bone, was certain that she had missed something not having lived through the Sixties, and, seeking a sense of verisimilitude, took up a collection of gold fillings and pace makers to auction on behalf of the newly formed Coalition Against Fore.

The money was not enough.

And on that one October evening, as the leaves began to fall creating a much-desired blanket against the impending cold, the kind of evening when the living should be sitting around a fire together, touching, chatting, or cheating at cards—by happenstance the very anniversary of the night Elvira Corona was bludgeoned to dead by her brother—Elvira, always reluctant to speak up, to see danger at her door, sat straight up in her grave, spouting a most stirring sermon about the lack of gravity of the cause and the hackneyed bluster of the misguided.

The bulldozers came.

And here our cemetery story stops, the bones shaken, even those of the previously discounted dead wife of her merry widower husband—who, if we could read into the future for a moment, would soon join his wife should they find her now unmarked grave, or if he would prefer, sleep for all eternity with the bones of the handsomely morrowed, newly widowed, blue-haired neighbor with whom he was currently cavorting in the flesh.

The clubhouse was built.

The dead, forgetting about their once harrowing cause, have learned to delight in the sound of the word *fore*, simply because of the shape it makes on the lips of the living, a shape that can be taken to suggest surprise, ecstasy, even horror.

In 8th Grade

I longed for breasts like Mary Berghope's;
they were the best breasts in our class,
proud and pointed forward like a ship's bow.

When she wore angora sweaters they
were more alive than they needed to be.
At recess they were our angry fists,
marshmallow-covered cupcakes at lunch.

The swirl and loop of Miss Rosscup's
careful cursive placed them on the blackboard;
the big hands of the clock traced them and
echoed the ticking of my shallow heart.

>Now I have cups so large, so reinforced
>they are skullcaps, ceremonial chalices,
>cantaloupe, summer squash.

>When Jenny called about her cancer
>I was too stunned to speak.
>After the call I crossed my arms
>over my chest like armour, a shield
>from fate and my petty covetousness.

When I Stand Watching

Wide faced hibiscus here,
unkempt hydrangea there,
I am the only thing
not blaring color,
not flagging the season.

(My buds plucked long ago
under the sterile light.)

When I stand here watching
my granddaughter touch her nose
to the Queen Anne's Lacey head…

(She tells me that they smell like
carrots. I tell her they smell like
licorice to me.)

Her back to me, feet rooted
to the second, she bends,
plucks off one lacy spiral,
as I wonder how I might
help her take this
sun-drenched sanctuary
into her old age.

UNTIL THEY FALL

The dentist says, "Oh, oh...," her hands in my mouth while her assistant holds the suction gun limp-wristed, like a pencil she might use for doodling if the mood strikes her.

"Look," the dentist continues, pointing with her rubber-gloved finger, the glove a faded turquoise (a color that does not appear in nature). "See that?"

"Um hum," the assistant nearly yawns the word, then pops her gum. *Should a dental assistant be chewing gum?*

"What do you see?" *Is this a quiz? Do they have time to use me as a prop?* "Looks like she is losing bone. Is that why the teeth are falling?"

Falling? Did she say falling? Would one of them look at my whole face please? I have a face.

My mouth has been pried open, painfully wide in an exaggerated O, like Maria Callas front and center in an articulation of sorrow.

What would I sing with my mouth so? O Solo Mio? A song my father used to sing. I hum it in the back of my throat. They think I want them to squirt water into my mouth.

I hold the water high in my throat and continue to hum. O Solo Mio, an easy tremolo, makes me think of water bubbling up from a dry spring bed.

"They are going to have to go," the dentist says, as if commenting on a pair of old loafers. She removes her hands and the utensils from my mouth and sits me up.

"I have bad news for you." She is smiling, a small smile like Mona Lisa gone sadistic. Sympathy is difficult for her. "You are going to have to lose two teeth, one right in front, the other further back. We can do that today if you have time."

I think, what if we were talking about a finger, would they be so cavalier? After all, there are nerves and blood vessels, then bone beneath the surface of that tooth. Like a finger, the tooth is a part of me. The tooth, more importantly is up front, on my face.

"What happens if I do nothing right now?" my words impossibly steady as I try not to cry.

I hear part of an answer as I rise from the chair, something about how the good teeth will shift. I think tectonic plates—earthquake—but at this very moment I don't care if the Rockies crumble. I remove the paper bib; tell her I will call her. I know that what I am doing will not stop the loss I must face. A loss. Not just a procedure. But not yet. The world spins, and I can't change that. I will decide what they take and when.

On the drive home I think of a day in middle school, one of the popular boys calling me "Bucky" because of the protrusion of my two large front teeth. Braces were never an option. Too expensive.

I have always been ashamed of my teeth, have always covered my mouth when I laugh, have always noticed other people's perfect smiles.

But now, I glance at myself in the rearview mirror, my face, eyes, nose, and mouth, a disembodied cameo in quicksilver, and suddenly, I love my face, my eyes, nose, all of my protruding, crooked teeth. I sing, (changing the lyrics a bit):
> Ma n'atu sole
> Chiu' bello oi ne'
> O solo mio
> E sul mio viso

I translate, not a perfect translation, for the dentist, for that boy:
> But another sun
> That's even brighter
> It's my own sun
> That's on my face.

My face. A face with funny, crooked, large teeth. And even if wrong-headed, I will keep these teeth just for now; will hold them like pearls when they fall.

"There is a fountain of youth; it is in your mind, your talent, the creativity you bring to you and the lives of people you love. When you learn to tap this source, you will truly have defeated age."

Sophia Loren

In June

It is turtles leaving
their weedy ponds;
noses, tiny arrowheads,
point toward
a providence of reed.

I take the back roads
to the post office; the pull
of sweet honeysuckle
makes me swoon, but I
keep my eyes on the dusty road—
a large snapper dead center.

I stop to move him across,
left hand on his perfect geometry,
right on his silky underside.
He stretches his leathery neck,
face in full war paint;
hisses unapologetically.

He doesn't know the difference
between danger and salvation.

I call him Shot Put
to add levity to the peril
we face together,
tell him he needs
to move faster if he
is to cross the road.

A driver in a passing car honks,
makes a curlicue with her finger
near her temple to tell me
I'm crazy; another
gives me the finger.

Then an older man
in a rusted pick-up

gives me a thumbs up.
He's not my type,
looks like Willie Nelson,
but I love him. I mean,
I could love him.
How would that work?

I imagine sitting in a beer joint
with the man, eating
stale beer nuts.
I convince him to buy
a Winnebago, to paint
"Turtle Rescue League"
on the sides.

We travel the back roads
saving turtles;
at night we park
near our favorite swamp,
delight in the guttural
plunk-twang of frogs,
slap at mosquitoes.

We buy night goggles to watch
the turtles lift their heads up
through the brackish stew,
take a moonlit breath, dive under.
I get West Nile virus, he
just drinks more beer.

AT THE TIRE REPAIR SHOP

I tell the young man—
his name tag says Joe—
that the pressure
in my new tires
goes low
every few days.

"Number?" he asks.

Does he mean the
number of tires,
the size of the tires,
my phone number?
He doesn't look up
but I can see his hands
arched, ready to poke
the keyboard with the tip
of his calloused fingers.

I give him my phone number.

"Keys," his voice a perfect D flat,
neither a question nor a request.

I give him my keys.
I have yet to see his eyes.
I suspect they are green or blue
because of his high cheek bones,
hair the color of almonds.
I am guessing Irish or German descent.

He takes my keys, finally looks up,
points with a curved arm
that makes me think of
a malleable toy
I played with as a child.

He says, "waiting room."
I want to ask,
what I am waiting for:
good fortune, a loss
not yet imagined?
The last diagnosis?

PEDICURE TIME

This is not aesthetics. I am old,
my feet are arthritic, old turtles.

I am flanked by young women.
One shows us her recent tongue piercings.
(Who would wound themselves on purpose?)

One 20-something is all *blah blah* about her baby's bowels.
Another 40ish is braying about her colicky husband.

I tell the girl to put lime green polish on my toenails.
Are you sure? she scans my face as she asks.

I am thinking of a poem by William Carlos Williams
about spring, about green mustaches.

The pedicurist's forehead is a two track,
but I can see a tulip sprouting from my toe.

THE YOUNG BARISTA

knows what I want before
I order, says, *Chai tea, right, Gloria?*
I look at his name tag—it is blank.
He sees me searching for his name,
tells me his name is *Nah-me-tagh*,
from the mystical land of Taghmenah.
A dusting of freckles like a sprinkling
of nutmeg across his forehead and chin
adds to his whimsy, his charm.

He is likely one-third my age,
and yet my heart goes rat-a-tat-tat,
a feeling I haven't had in years.
I rake my unruly bangs down to cover
forehead wrinkles, relieved
that I am wearing sunglasses
that hide dark circles under my eyes.

The older barista chimes in
with *Gloria-Gloria-Gloria, I think*
we got your number. A song
I remember from the 80s.
A woman in line near my age sings,
Gloria, G-L-O R-I A, she comes
around here just about midnight.
I tell her that the guys who served
on the Coast Guard Cutter Bramble
used to sing that version of "Gloria" to me.

Her eyebrows lift and stretch
like escaping caterpillars. Still, I continue,
"I dated two of the guys from the Cutter
(yes, at the same time), liked one guy
better than the other, just felt sorry
for sailor number two—lonely soul.
Then, one day while I stood on the dock
waiting for one of them, they both

came walking down the gang plank
together. I waved—hand held close
to my beating, cheating heart—
then I quickly took leave."

The next time I see the young barista,
I ask, "Nah-me-tagh, how are you?"
"Three jobs," he says, "exhausted."
"It gets better," I say.
But I am lying. It got worse—
house…kids…husband…career…
(unfortunately, in that order).

The young barista smiles,
makes me look into the respite
of his clear-sky-blue eyes. And
as he turns away, I notice
his broad shoulders, notice
his tight, muscled back
like gathered manila rope, rope
that might secure an anchor.

And while my head is a swirl
of sweeter words, inappropriate words,
all I manage is, "Have a good day."
Still, I know what I might have been
in a distant time, an unforgiving place.

For safekeeping, I put myself on a chair
in the farthest corner of the café,
my back to the young baristas. Still
the sounds of dripping water,
rattling ice, exasperated hissing
of the frothing gadget mark
just where he is, where I am not.

After a deep sigh, I sip my
expensive drink, curse all time
and order—but just the same,
I suddenly feel happily ridiculous.

I Join Them

I do not want a plain box
I want a sarcophagus...
                    Sylvia Plath

In a cab the color of summer squash,
Sylvia places words on her fingers
like skewers and offers them
to the men who pass along Fifth Avenue.
The driver asks, "The meter, ladies,
where we goin'?"
"To the womb to stay warm," Anne says.

A pile of phrases sits on my lap.
I try a few:
          "On the spot.
          Into the world.
          For life."
And together we laugh
at the gravity of something
as incomplete as a phrase.

I look closely at the poets' faces
the way I might inspect
a lady slipper, an orchid,
the skin fresh with dew,
that will first wither, then die.

I look out at the city, watch
the sewer steam lift,
then dissipate like a sigh.

Hugs

My grandchildren hug me
quickly, like a game of tag;
my dog attempts a hug, paws
on my shoulders, knobby head
into my capable chest.

(The cat has more success;
her hazardous paws pull me in.)

But no one has hugged me
with romantic intent in years,
just the platonic bump
of arms and shoulders,
a peck on the cheek.

As a pre-teen
I kissed my pillow,
or the cushion of flesh
where thumb attaches
web-like to finger,

wrapped my nighttime
blanket into a long, lean specter,
gave the headless roll
a name: Dwayne,
Gary, Eddie Gotchlink.

And in my dreams
Elvis hugged me.
Ricky Nelson.
The boy behind the counter
at the five and dime.

Once a teen,
a different problem:
first boys, then men, wanted
to touch. Not with two arms;
they didn't have time for that.

Even an older cousin
tried to touch here—there,
but by then I was adept
at twisting and twirling,
a ballerina in the shadows.

As I sit here today
in what some call dotage,
I don't know if I should be
dismayed or grateful
for my near hug-less life,

knowing as we all must
that touch can bruise,
that the cost of every hug
harbors the question
of intent—leads to the finality
of turning away.

COME CHILD, I AM WAITING

After the bang, the swirling dust,
from a single starting point,
cell, sea creature,
changeling mudskipper,
mammoth, mastodon,
extinction, mutation all around
still you come…

50,000 years ago,
deep in a cave in France,
you took gypsum to stone,
etched in the near dark
the majesty of the creatures
you could not name.

Up from a barren place,
from the lush and teeming,
from tribe and terrain,
from the shadow
of this victory and that,
proud Roman with shield,
with ideas, slaves,
you come—
cold war, hot war, this war, the next,
brewing in the bloody dreams
of vengeful old men,
indiscriminate, teeming microbes,
a curse on all,
still you come…

In the acrid hold with steerage,
dirges spinning you round, dizzy,
beneath the lighted torch
as they search your head for lice
and you bow to the indignity
because you must come,
you come.

I listen for bells—
steeple bells,
bells of merriment,
funeral tolling,
tintantibulation for
the old poet left searching
for the descant toll.

From the chaliced holding,
from the guessing place,
place of the great circle,
swirling, weaving—
you come. And I am waiting.

First a pearly swaddle,
the inside of the swirled shell.
Filmy wet, we lift you up,
expect to see ourselves
but you come,
your fists, odd January buds,
opening to take up the scribed
and uninscribed destiny.
Out of pain and expectation
you come. In the finite moment,
you come to this one place
where I stand waiting.

GRANDMA

is over there at the edge
of the flower garden.
If you look in her direction
she will see you—she is
always looking for you.

She will try to call you closer,
tell you that the sun is warmer
where she is rooted, that the bird
songs are sweeter there. But

you are content to think
about that one boy at school
and the song you heard
when he drove away
on a rainy night in April.

Unable to sleep, you recall
the little dog that used to crawl
into bed with you once everyone
else in the house was asleep.

Lately your head pounds
when you think about life's
incongruities, how desire
is eclipsed by obligation.

No time to think about Grandma
where she once stood, beyond
the more decorous perennials,
arms held open like a welcoming saint.

In twenty years or so you,
when you think about her,
will wonder when you last saw her.
Then suddenly you will think about
the question she waited
for you to ask.

IF I AM EVER IN A COMA

For Renee

If I am ever in a coma, tweeze my eyebrows,
my mustache and chin hairs. I don't want
to look like Groucho or Freda…neither is a role model.
Clip my toenails, though doing so might require power tools.

Ask Shelly Smith to color my hair. Tell her, *up a notch*,
she will know what that means. Share
one of your deepest regrets with her, and she
will texture it with her able hands,
will curl her heart around it.

I don't have to tell you to feed the cats,
dogs and horses; their dependence is obvious,
but don't forget the birds—hang suet and fill feeders.
The hummingbirds will come in April or May;
they will come and will worship your gesture.

When the young doctors tell you that I am brain dead,
that you should pull the plug, flip the switch, *let me go,*
tell them that I have rich relatives who contribute
large sums to the hospital. Do your homework,
have names at the ready. They are skeptics.

My dog Jazz likes to play. She will let you know when,
will posture herself for joy, will hold the red ball
in her mouth like a gift. Take it. Throw it.
She will always bring it back to you.

I should have said this first: go immediately
to my underwear drawer, throw the ragged contents away,
leave the lavender sachet. I will buy only silk and lace
from this point forward, in this life or the next.

Take my jewelry, take all of it. I don't want you
to see another woman wearing it. Don't wait
for permission—go now! Take it. All of it.

Spend some time snooping. Look for my transgressions,
my secrets—doing so will entertain you, help you.
Forgive yourself for anything you have done, might do.
Don't forget to call the relatives in Italy, tell them
that I am critical. They will anoint themselves,
will kneel in the filigreed halls,
will say those long-beaded prayers.

God forbid, if I don't survive the coma,
see my poem, *Once I am Dead*—it begins
with the instructions: *Use the words Liberal
and Democrat in my eulogy, no matter
how some will protest.*

It's All Too Much

Eyes going opaque,
teeth chipping, falling,
hips and toes collapsing.

My dead father's hats
on a hook in the hall.

No comfort from Buddhist,
Peppiest, acolytes of any stripe,
their ceremonial smoke
just another stink, and so—

        bones of today
        I am going to leave you
        under the sunflower's
        hanging black eye.
        Some will attempt
        to grow skin for me—
        the reptilian Haworthia will try.

        The nightshades will offer me limbs.

        But only the moonflower
        with its sturdy stalk, webbed hands,
        will form muscle, and it will reach
                for me in this, my darkest hour.

About the Author

Gloria (Demasi) Nixon-John earned an M.A. in Rhetoric and Journalism from Wayne State University in Detroit and a Ph.D. in English from Michigan State University. She has published poems, fiction, and essays as well as pedagogical chapters and articles for teachers. Her dissertation work focuses on Canadian poet, Bronwen Wallace. Gloria's novel, *The Killing Jar,* is based on the true story of one of the youngest Americans to have served on death row. Her memoir, *Learning from Lady Chatterley,* is written in narrative verse and set in post-WWII Detroit. Her chapbook, *Breathe me a Sky*, was published by The Moonstone Arts Center of Philadelphia.

Gloria has taught English and Speech in grades 8-12 as well as Teacher Education courses at Michigan State University. She is a Red Cedar Writing Project (Michigan State University) Teacher Consultant. Gloria has collected an oral history of sculptor Marshall Fredericks for the Marshall Fredricks Museum in Saginaw, Michigan, and has done oral history work for the Theodore Roethke House, also in Saginaw, Michigan. She currently works as an independent writing consultant for schools, libraries and individual writers. Gloria lives in rural Oxford, Michigan, with her horses, dogs, cats, and husband Michael.

ACKNOWLEDGMENTS:

To my brother, Vince, who will recognize some of the events that prompted these poems, but he will remember it all differently—as older brothers do. To my husband, Michael, who tolerates my emotional meandering. To my cheering squad: Renee H. Nixon, Jaimie Ward, April and Angelina Wiater, and Colleen Barkham.

A heartfelt thanks to Anita Skeen and Marilyn Wilson at Michigan State University for their help and encouragement. To Michael Steinberg and Ruth Nathan, who gave me opportunities in Michigan's writing community. To Terry Blackhawk and the students and staff of InsideOut in Detroit. Thanks to Annie Ransford and the Theodore Roethke House for workshop opportunities, and Wilma Romantz, artist and cohort in creative endeavors. To Steven Dunn, who taught me the difference between a good poem and the not-so-good. I bow to Canadian poet Browen Wallace, who left us too soon but left her poems behind.

Bless you, Stacy Parker LeMelle, Director of First Person Plural of Harlem, who includes me, her old teacher, in FPP events. A special thanks to poet and friend Holly Hughes, editor and poet par excellence. To the Moonstone Arts Center of Philadelphia and A3 of London as they saw value in my work. Last, I am shouting now to Judy Kerman of Mayapple Press for her astute and clearheaded guidance.

RECENT TITLES FROM MAYAPPLE PRESS

Nancy Takacs, *Dearest Water*, 2022
    Paper, 84pp, 19.95 plus s&h
    ISBN: 978-1-952781-09-4
Zilka Joseph, *In Our Beautiful Bones*, 2021
    Paper, 108pp, $19.95 plus s&h
    ISBN: 9780-1-952781-07-0
Ricardo Jesús Mejías Hernández, tr. Don Cellini, *Libro de Percances/Book of Mishaps*, 2021
    Paper, 56pp, $18.95 plus s&h
    ISBN: 978-952781-05-6
Eleanor Lerman, *Watkins Glen*, 2021
    Paper, 218pp, $22.95 plus s&h
    ISBN: 978-1-952781-01-8
Betsy Johnson, *when animals are animals*, 2021
    Paper, 58pp, $17.95 plus s&h
    ISBN: 978-1-952781-02-5
Jennifer Anne Moses, *The Man Who Loved His Wife*, 2021
    Paper, 172pp, $20.95 plus s&h
    ISBN: 978-1-936419-96-8
Judith Kunst, *The Way Through*, 2020
    Paper, 76pp, $17.95 plus s&h
    ISBN: 978-1-936419-98-2
Ellen Stone, *What Is in the Blood*, 2020
    Paper, 72pp, $17.95 plus s&h
    ISBN 978-1-936419-95-1
Terry Blackhawk, *One Less River*, 2019
    Paper, 78pp, $16.95 plus s&h
    ISBN 978-1-936419-89-0
Ellen Cole, *Notes from the Dry Country*, 2019
    Paper, 88pp, $16.95 plus s&h
    ISBN 978-1-936419-87-6
Monica Wendel, *English Kills and other poems*, 2018
    Paper, 70pp, $15.95 plus s&h
    ISBN 978-1-936419-84-5

For a complete catalog of Mayapple Press publications, please visit our website at *www.mayapplepress.com*. Books can be ordered direct from our website with secure on-line payment using PayPal, or by mail (check or money order). Or order through your local bookseller.